HOME SERIES

HOME SERIES
BEDROOMS

BETA-PLUS

CONTENTS

P. 4-5
A creation by the interior architect Marijke Van Nunen.

P. 6
Floral motifs, but in a contemporary atmosphere for this bedroom in a house by the architect Stany Dietvors.

INTRODUCTION

The bourgeoisie were responsible for separating the bedroom from the other rooms of day-to-day life to become a room in its own right at the end of the 18th century.

Now a separate, intimate area, it is the cocoon of the house. Interior designers and their clients pay more and more attention to this refuge. The current trend is therefore to create truly private areas with a suite for parents, an en suite bathroom and separate dressing room in order to leave a space free exclusively for rest.

Rest and relaxation have not been forgotten: numerous bedrooms also have a living room corner with comfortable sofas and sometimes even a television area.

This book presents some thirty highly sought-after bedrooms, created by renowned designers and interior architects: every style is here, from classical to minimalism, from romantic to designer chic and from rustic to the resolutely contemporary.

In spite of their great diversity, all these creations have several things in common: the sense of space, the harmony of colour and the passion for refined materials and fabrics.

P. 8
An Esther Gutmer creation.

P. 10-11
This room was created by the Cy Peys/Partners architect's practice. White-painted pine panelling.

TIMELESS REFINEMENT

T his section presents four bedrooms devised by the designer Walda Pairon.

Her characteristic style is apparent, where a harmony of colours, fabrics and materials dominates.

A controlled mix of antique and contemporary for rooms that are simultaneously modern and timeless.

P. 14-15
The doors are glazed with antique glass panes.
The floorboards extend from the bedroom to the dressing room.
A 17th century wooden Madonna stands on a small table from the same period.

P. 16-17
In this classic bedroom, Walda Pairon has chosen to combine valuable objects and antique furniture (a walnut cabinet, a sheep bone seat, rare horn tumblers and decanters, etc.), silky fabrics and a fitted carpet in pure new wool.

P. 18-19
The paying guest room in the same dwelling with its own rather understated charm.

P. 20-21
Stronger colouring and a muffled atmosphere for the guest room, with antique English bedside tables, pleated lampshades, a 19th century writing desk and antique prints.

THREE CONTEMPORARY

GUEST ROOMS

S lapen enzo is an outstanding Bed & Breakfast in Antwerp.

With the help of the Cotwee design bureau, the owners have transformed this average building into an elegant dwelling infused with luxury and comfort.

The three guest rooms, with a real designer look, are themed by colour – a resolutely modern, simple approach for a confident decorative effect.

P. 22-23
The dark room extends over two floors, offering an intimate setting for the occupants. The dark colours create a muffled, luxurious atmosphere.

P. 24-25
The white room is infused with calm, simplicity and purity.

P. 26-27
The mocca room (decorated in brown tones) has a very warm, reassuring atmosphere.

ROMANTIC INSPIRATION

IN AN OLD POST HOUSE

L ocated in the historic heart of Bruges, the Relais Bourgon-disch Cruyce draws the eye with its half-timbered façade. It is known as one of the most romantic luxury hotels in Europe.

The recently refurbished rooms of this unusual hotel offer refined decoration while remaining snug and comfortable, embellished with stylish furniture. The two rooms presented in this section were designed and fitted out by Brigitte Garnier.

P. 28-29
The walls of the room are panelled in aged oak. The bed, a Garnier piece, is made of oak (the same model is also available in mahogany). An 18th century French console table is set beautifully against the wall. The fabrics are Ralph Lauren.

The television and minibar are built into the wardrobes.
The spotlights are designed by Jan Van den Hove, available from Garnier in bronze, brass and chrome.

Attic room in light colours, decorated with Ralph Lauren fabrics throughout.

COLOURFUL UNDERSTATEMENT

nterior architect Nathalie Van Reeth wanted to give this coastal apartment a calming atmosphere for a family with children.

The apartment consists of an open space, which includes the kitchen, living room and dining room.

The bedrooms have been handled in a simple and playful manner: immaculate white dominates, brightened up with a few lively, dynamic touches of colour.

P. 32-33

The corridor leading to the bedrooms dares to be colourful, in bright red softened by the subdued light and the low, built-in spotlights.

The white communication doors pivot and run from floor to ceiling. The grey floorboards cover the whole of the apartment in a natural material, contrasting with the gloss-finish MDF cupboards. These made-to-measure features provide an additional storage space. The room decoration is understated and light. The white fabric blinds and the colourful accents create a quiet yet lively ensemble.

P. 34-35
Above the bed, a photo by
Verne (from Items).

PRIDE OF PLACE

In the historic heart of Antwerp, two mansions have been restored by AID Architects to create an exceptional place to stay; Hôtel Julien.

The rooms have been entirely rearranged to create eleven spacious hotel rooms with superb bathrooms. The open patio creates a meeting point between the two buildings and creates light and space in the rooms. As part of the restoration, the key historic elements have been preserved and given pride of place. The addition of large picture windows on the ground floor and in the stairwells made it possible to accentuate the consistency with the interior garden, making the whole ensemble into a very open and airy building.

The rooms are understated and neutral tones dominate, allowing the original architectural features to be emphasised, particularly the beams and fireplaces.

P. 38-39

A timeless modern symbiosis of old rooms full of character, made to measure contemporary elements and designer furniture. Linen and natural cotton fabrics. Antique oak floor.

P. 40-41
Beamed ceiling bearing the original paint texture and painted bark between the beams.

P. 42 and below
The interior decoration focuses on understated lines and colours, accentuating the existing architecture and historical details.

The wall cabinet, made to measure, houses a TV, DVD player, minibar, clothes rail and desk, all with integral indirect lighting.

BEDROOMS WITH CHARACTER

n this section, Dutch interior architect Bert Quadvlieg presents the bedrooms he created in a country house in Théoule-sur-Mer and in a holiday home in Grasse.

As is often the case, he draws his inspiration from sustainable materials, lively colours and antique-inspired furniture to create a harmonious whole.

These bedrooms are all confidently decorated, whether the inspiration is exotic or more classical.

P. 44-47
The bamboo canopied four-poster bed
is the realisation of a Quadvlieg design.
The dressing room doors are covered in
leather and bamboo. Desk with
Scagliola marble inlay (Italy, 17th
century).

P. 48-49
The wrought iron canopied four-poster bed was designed by Quadvlieg. The majority of the fabrics are by Ralph Lauren.

The walls, painted with a lined motif, have been created using several layers.
Bamboo floor covering.

The mirror frame was made using shells from Portugal and the Maldives.

The canopy and headboard are Quadvlieg creations. Light pink and cream fabrics by Ralph Lauren.

The head of the bed and the seat are both covered in an authentic kilim. An early 18th century French table stands next to the wall. The mosquito net is made from an old grain sieve.

The antique wrought iron bed comes from Florence. Oak floor.

The head of the bed bears an oak decoration that was initially located above a double door. The unbleached fabrics are from Italy.

The canopied four-poster bed is made of patinaed mahogany. Floral wallpaper by Ralph Lauren. Above the desk are two framed pieces of Chinese calligraphy.

P. 54-55
The sandstone fireplace comes from Helena Rubinstein's villa. The original terracotta floor (from around 1950) is the only flooring that has been preserved in this country house. Wallpaper and fabrics by Ralph Lauren.

DISCREET LUXURY

nterior architect Gilles de Meulemeester and his design company Ebony have become unmissable points of reference when it comes to interior design, with boutiques in Brussels and Paris.

From renovation to pure design, Gilles de Meulemeester is responsible for the design of numerous private residences in Belgium, Paris, the south of France, London, Geneva, Berlin, Moscow and even Aspen in the United States.

The project in this section reveals a chic, contemporary air. Highly refined materials and colours mark this discreetly luxurious bedroom.

P. 58-61
Alongside its interior design service, Ebony can suggest various collections of furniture, decorative items and accessories.

A CONTEMPORARY AIR

IN A RESTORED CASTLE

Vittorio Simoni's office took on the task of the interior design for the whole of this restored castle.

Simoni transformed the vaulted cellars into a true oasis of calm and well-being.

The bedrooms in this unique project also display serenity and contemporary classic elegance, shown especially by the colour range chosen: brown, beige, dove-grey, etc.

Jozef Reynaerts designed the wallpaper and decorative coverings.

P. 62-63
The entrance hall and access to the bathroom are embellished by dark tinted oak floorboards.
The dressing room cupboards are also in oak veneer, tinted the same shade as the floorboards.
On the lower level, the bedroom has tinted oak skirting around a Van Besouw carpet.

P. 64-65

Two bedrooms with their accompanying bathrooms.
The floors are in dark tinted oak floorboards. The oak-veneered furniture
has been tinted the same colour as the floorboards (Williams & Koch).
A Duravit basin was chosen for the bathroom.
The paintings are in stucco and a play of indirect lighting and built-in
Kreon spotlights has been created to warm the atmosphere.
The old radiators have been preserved.

P. 66-67

The owners' bedroom. A dresser acts as
a demarcation between the bedroom
and the transit area, at the same time
as providing storage. Promemoria
lamps.

SOOTHING SHADING

This bedroom, designed by Sophie Campion, is decorated in teak to produce aquatic green colour shading in linen, silk and cotton. Artworks by José Maria Sicilia, Robert Mapplethorpe and Andreas Schön.

A natural air for a soothing bedroom.

EQUILIBRIUM AND CLEAN LINES

B ased on balanced proportions and clean lines, the contemporary spirit – simultaneously modern and timeless – of XVL Home Collection reveals the beauty and sensuality of an interior.

This collection, created by Xavier Van Lil and made to measure in oak or wenge, leaves the material in its simplest form of expression.

XVL furniture unites purity and modernity, as shown by this depiction of a suite of bedrooms produced by XVL.

P. 72 73
A bedroom with an almost masculine
elegance: dark woods and austere lines
for a Zen atmosphere.

CONTRASTING COLOURS

AND MATERIALS

This bedroom design by Simone Kengo (Minimal Interior) illustrates her work on contrasts in colours and materials.

Cream versus ebony, velvet versus linen; materials and colours that, juxtaposed with one another, bring each other to prominence: the silkiness and preciousness of the velvet are reinforced when placed alongside raw, natural linen.

A delicate task, with an elegant result.

P. 74-75

The leather-handled chest of drawers and the bed frame are in silk-finish mocha oak (Catherine Memmi). Bed cover in taupe velvet. Bartholomeus linen rug. The dressing room (p. 74) was made to measure.

A 1930S STYLE BED/SITTING ROOM

n an apartment in the style of a 1935 ocean liner, the interior architect Mario Bruyneel has worked closely with the owner to create a space that perfectly exemplifies modern comfort and pays homage to the inter-war period and the Art Deco style.

P. 76-77

Sycamore furniture and bevelled plate glass chest of drawers. Night lights by Jacques Adnet. The contrasting "Chinese Dragon" panels by O&L have been used as the headboard. A Mario Bruyneel creation.

RELAXED COMFORT

I n this house, the bedrooms are decorated with a harmonious ensemble of old and new: characterful antique objects and furniture highlighted by a few contemporary notes and Orac mouldings.

The natural materials and fabrics used put the finishing touches on the décor. Snugly comfortable rooms in a relaxed atmosphere.

Linen blinds and a bleached oak table between salvaged shutters. Louis XV-style sofa with a canework back and seat covered in linen by Libeco. Skirting and mouldings from the Orac Decor collection.

Sisal fitted carpet and aubergine-coloured walls. Antique standing mannequin. The doors were made with frames from the Orac Decor collection.

A George II-style oak stool under a French hunting scene.

The walls of this girl's bedroom have been decorated in two colours: an Orac Axxent moulding emphasises the separation.

P. 82
English tables either side of the bed. Behind, a George III mahogany chest of drawers between a Napoleon III stool and a Louis XV-style armchair. On the chest of drawers, various English-style accessories and wooden boxes.

UNDERSTATEDNESS,

SUSTAINABILITY, AUTHENTICITY

T he decorator Alexandra Siebe-link has devised an original play on old and new materials to create a serene, modern atmosphere. No superfluous embellishments, but rather understated, sustainable materials that radiate true warmth and authenticity.

The rustic style is revisited and given clean lines in this bedroom that provides a good illustration of the decorator's philosophy. A symphony of whites brings lightness into the room, in spite of the strong presence of beams. These white-painted beams now form a reassuring alcove.

GUEST BEDROOMS

IN A CENTURIES-OLD CASTLE

S pycker castle dates back to the 12th century. In 1873, it was completely renovated in the fin de siècle style. The outside of the castle has the typical character of the new renaissance; the inside is entirely decorated in the style of Napoleon III.

Spycker castle was recently completely restored thanks to two antique dealer couples who previously worked in the hotel sector: the Van Haecke and De Clerck families.

They took care to preserve the original architectural elements (plaster moul-dings, doors, false floors, marble floors, etc.). The castle is now a residence, a private showroom for antiques and exclu-sive fabrics, and an ideal place to wel-come guests.

It has stylish bedrooms, all characterised by refinement and elegance.

P. 86-91
The three paying guest rooms of the castle were designed by Frederik De Clerck with exclusive printed fabrics by Bracquenié and Pierre Frey, taffeta by Métaphores, quilts by Elsa C. and furniture from the castle's superb collection of antiquities.

WORTHY OF A SUITE

This bedroom, designed by Sphere Interiors, has been treated like a luxury hotel suite, with a dressing room, bathroom and TV corner.

The guiding principle was understated, contemporary decoration. A palette of soft, subtle tints in various shades of beige contrasts with the furniture pieces in dark wood.

The result: a discreetly luxurious bedroom.

P. 92-93

Nilson bed, Piet Boon headboard. Behind the bed, a television support. The sofa was made to measure. Dressing room: fitted carpet placed on an under-carpet. Surrounded by made to measure cupboards.

TIMELESS BEDROOMS

T he three Flamant brothers and their team have a passion for interior decoration and design, creating objects and furniture that feel as though they have always been there.

Flamant Home Interiors has developed a concept that is both simple and clever: reusing old furniture and objects adapted to today's needs. A mix of styles and inspirations from old England to the exoticism of the colonies, in Scandinavian and Provençal styles.

The lines, however, remain very modern.

All the bedrooms in this section illustrate these styles in a contemporary way, free of a 'total look' concept. These are styles that have been revisited and reinterpreted.

Cape Cod four-poster bed in white, with a matching stool. Flamant bed linen and throw.

Sleigh bed and wardrobe painted white, in the style of Louis XVI.

P. 96-97
Flamant always succeeds in blending elements from different cultures and styles into a harmonious, timeless whole.

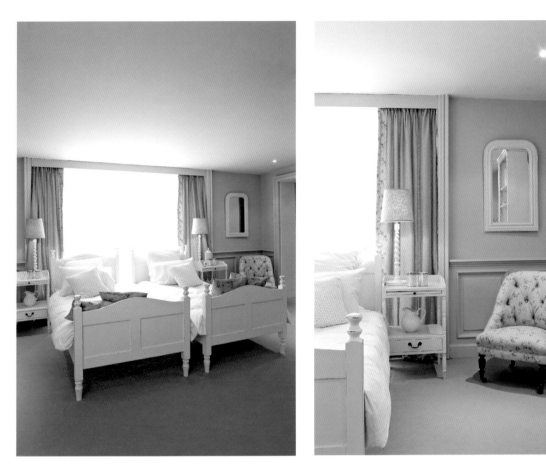

P. 98-99
The world of Flamant is a world of discreet luxury and intimate charm. It offers the perfect combination of customisation, comfort and innovation.

SHEEN OF CENTURIES

T his section depicts two bedrooms and the upstairs landing of a square farmhouse restored and redesigned inside by sisters Virginie and Odile Dejaegere, renowned designers.

Muted, reduced tones envelop these rooms and create a very intimate world that is both snug and reassuring.

P. 100-103
In this huge farmhouse, each room has its own character. Thanks to old painting techniques, the choice of a variety of antique objects and the ancient oak flooring (Van Huele), the bedrooms have an atmosphere of days gone by.

NATURAL MATERIALS

VERSUS CLEAN LINES

The interior architect Isabelle Bijvoet devised the design with its understated lines for this light-filled room. The interior shutters allow filtered lighting to be created where the shade complements and accentuates the contemporary edge of the place.

The wenge veneered wardrobes are cleverly built into the width of the walls, freeing up space. The whole ensemble is approached with a certain austerity and suggests a rather masculine interior.

P. 104-107
The interlinked oak floor and the understated nature of the palette create an atmosphere marked by serenity. Isabelle Bijvoet also designed the furniture to measure, while the accessories are second-hand.

CALM AND UNDERSTATEMENT

T his section presents two recent bedroom creations designed by interior architect Philip Simoen.

Simoen's stamp is readily apparent on both projects: an understated palette, a soothing atmosphere and a preference for natural, sustainable fabrics and materials.

P. 110-111
The MDF wall covering has been whitewashed and varnished.
Maxalto armchairs (Citterio), Lenti and Hermès throws. The bed cover fabric is from Zimmer & Rhode. Larsen rug and Nogushi bedside lamps. Modo wooden blinds.

Aged oak panelling and wardrobes. Malabar bed cover and
Flos wall lamps, designed by Starck.

P. 112
In this bedroom in an
apartment on the Belgian
coast, the wall behind the
bed is clad in horizontal oak
sheets for a graphical,
opulent effect. Bed cover
and curtains in a fabric by
Malabar. Bedside lamps by
Casamilano.

Wardrobes with a
painted MDF façade
and oak inside.
Bathroom tiling by
Dominique Desimpel.

ARTISANAL TRADITION

The artisan-style doors and windows of this bedroom were created by E. De Prins, a carpentry workshop with a sense of tradition maintained over two generations.

The lighting, furniture and frames were designed by AID Architects. Their approach: a simply decorated bedroom that is not overloaded; neutral, light colours for a light-filled, snug space.

The sash windows are locally made.

P. 116-117
The panelled doors with retro handles
were created by E. De Prins.

AN ATTIC GUEST SUITE

A young family with four children renovated this country house, located in an idyllic setting, turning it into a spacious, original dwelling.

They created a guest suite under the roof of the annexe building, housing a spacious bedroom with its own en suite bathroom, dressing room and a small living room. The whole ensemble has a timeless charm, accentuated by a very subtle harmony of colours. The smoothness of the paintings, achieved through the matt finish, adds a feeling of comfort and softness to this interior.

P. 118-121
The suite has been fitted out with
Flamant furniture and accessories. The
paintings are also from Flamant.
A sisal fitted carpet and a Vi-Spring
bed. The wall lights and the desk lamp
were made to measure by Stéphane
Donners. Painting by Walter Vilain.
Cupboard made to measure by JCB in
Spanish wood.

HOME SERIES

Volume 14 : BEDROOMS

The reports in this book are selected from the Beta-Plus collection of home-design books: www.betaplus.com
They have been compiled in a special series by Le Figaro in French language: Ma Déco

Copyright © 2009 Beta-Plus Publishing / Le Figaro
Originally published in French language

PUBLISHER
Beta-Plus Publishing
Termuninck 3
B – 7850 Enghien
Belgium
www.betaplus.com
info@betaplus.com

TEXT
Alexandra Druesne

PHOTOGRAPHY
Jo Pauwels

DESIGN
Polydem - Nathalie Binart

TRANSLATIONS
Txt-Ibis

ISBN: 978-90-8944-045-7

Printed in China

P. 124-125
One of the many bedrooms in a castle renovated by the
Simoni architect's practice.

P. 126-127
An Olivier Lempereur creation. Utterly contemporary austerity
and dark colours for a chic air.